P9-CBC-262

Southern Middle Media
5235 Solomon's Island Rd.
Lothian, MD 20711
WITHDRAWN

THE ORIGINAL UNITED STATES OF AMERICA

Americans Discover the Meaning of Independence 1770-1800

TITLE LIST

THE ORIGINAL UNITED STATES OF AMERICA:
Americans Discover the Meaning of Independence 1770-1800

BY
SHEILA NELSON

MASON CREST PUBLISHERS
PHILADELPHIA

Mason Crest Publishers Inc.
370 Reed Road
Broomall, Pennsylvania 19008
(866) MCP-BOOK (toll free)

Copyright © 2005 by Mason Crest Publishers. All rights reserved. No part of this publication may be reproduced or transmitted in any form or by any means, electronic or mechanical, including photocopying, recording, taping, or any information storage and retrieval system, without permission from the publisher.

First printing
1 2 3 4 5 6 7 8 9 10

Library of Congress Cataloging-in-Publication Data

Nelson, Sheila.
 The original United States of America : Americans discover the meaning of independence / by Sheila Nelson.
   p. cm. — (How America became America)
 Includes bibliographical references and index.
 Audience: Grades 9–12.
 ISBN 1-59084-903-5   ISBN 1-59084-900-0 (series)
 1. United States—Politics and government—1775–1783—Juvenile literature. 2. United States—Politics and government—1783–1789—Juvenile literature. 3. United States—History—Revolution, 1775–1783—Juvenile literature. 4. United States—History—Colonial period, ca. 1600–1775—Juvenile literature. I. Title. II. Series.
 E302.1.N43 2005
 973.3—dc22
                        2004015270

Design by M.K. Bassett-Harvey.
Produced by Harding House Publishing Service, Inc.
Cover design by Dianne Hodack.
Printed in the Hashemite Kingdom of Jordan.

CONTENTS

INTRODUCTION

by Dr. Jack Rakove

Today's America is not the same geographical shape as the first American colonies—and the concept of America has evolved as well over the years.

When the thirteen original states declared their independence from Great Britain, most Americans still lived within one or two hours modern driving time from the Atlantic coast. In other words, the Continental Congress that approved the Declaration of Independence on July 4, 1776, was continental in name only. Yet American leaders like George Washington, Benjamin Franklin, and Thomas Jefferson also believed that the new nation did have a continental destiny. They expected it to stretch at least as far west as the Mississippi River, and they imagined that it could extend even further. The framers of the Federal Constitution of 1787 provided that western territories would join the Union on equal terms with the original states. In 1803, President Jefferson brought that continental vision closer to reality by purchasing the vast Louisiana Territory from France. In the 1840s, negotiations with Britain and a war with Mexico brought the United States to the Pacific Ocean.

This expansion created great opportunities, but it also brought serious costs. As Americans surged westward, they created a new economy of family farms and large plantations. But between the Ohio River and the Gulf of Mexico, expansion also brought the continued growth of plantation slavery for millions of African Americans. Political struggle over the extension of slavery west of the Mississippi was one of the major causes of the Civil War that killed hundreds of thousands of Americans in the 1860s but ended with the destruction of slavery. Creating opportunities for American farmers also meant displacing Native Americans from the lands their ancestors had occupied for centuries. The opening of the west encouraged massive immigration not only from Europe but also from Asia, as Chinese workers came to labor in the California Gold Rush and the building of the railroads.

By the end of the nineteenth century, Americans knew that their great age of territorial expansion was over. But immigration and the growth of modern industrial cities continued to change the American landscape. Now Americans moved back and forth across the continent in search of economic opportunities. African Americans left the South in massive numbers and settled in dense concentrations in the cities of the North. The United States remained a magnet for immigration, but new immigrants came increasingly from Mexico, Central America, and Asia.

Ever since the seventeenth century, expansion and migration across this vast landscape have shaped American history. These books are designed to explain how this process has worked. They tell the story of how modern America became the nation it is today.

The TIMES are Dreadful Doleful Difmal Dolorous, and DOLLAR-LESS.

Thurfday, October 31. 1765

NUME 1195

THE PENNSYLVANIA JOURNAL;
AND
WEEKLY ADVERTISER.

EXPIRING: In Hopes of a Refurrection to LIFE again.

I am forry to be obliged to acquaint my readers that as the Stamp Act is feared to be obligatory upon us after the *firft of November* enfuing (The Fatal To-morrow), The publifher of this paper, unable to bear the Burthen, has thought it expedient to ftop awhile, in order to deliberate, whether any methods can be found to elude the chains forged for us, and efcape the infupportable flavery, which it is hoped, from the laft reprefentation now made againft that act, may be effected. Mean while I muft earneftly Requeft every individual of my Subfcribers, many of whom have been long behind Hand, that they would immediately difcharge their refpective Arrears, that I may be able, not only to fupport myfelf during the Interval, but be better prepared to proceed again with this Paper whenever an opening for that purpofe appears, which I hope will be foon.

WILLIAM BRADFORD.

Stamp Act protest

One
THE AMERICAN COLONIES' SENSE OF WHO THEY WERE

When the news of the proposed Stamp Act reached the American colonies, colonists gathered in shocked groups, discussing the outrage. They were British citizens! How dare **Parliament** insult them this way, taxing them without their consent! They looked incredulously at the text of the Stamp Act again; page after page it went on, listing the documents Parliament intended to tax. Soon, they would need to buy Parliament's stamps for every legal document, **bill of lading**, and university diploma. Even things like newspapers, calendars, playing cards, and dice would be taxed.

In 1765, the year Parliament unanimously passed the Stamp Act, the American colonists still thought of themselves as loyal British subjects. Most of them had come from the British Isles—England, Wales, Scotland, and Ireland—although thousands of people had arrived from other parts of Europe as well.

Colonists thought of America as an extension of Britain, even though their mother country was more than three thousand miles away. British governors, appointed by the king, ruled the colonies, and even when the colonists made their own laws, the king and Parliament had the right to override those laws and

Parliament is the governing body of Great Britain and is made up of the House of Commons and the House of Lords.

A bill of lading is a receipt listing the goods being shipped.

make others. As a part of Britain, the colonists expected the same rights as British citizens had back in Europe.

More than one and a half million people lived in the American colonies in the 1760s. They had come to the New World for many different reasons. Some wanted to explore and study the new land. Some wanted to make money from America's resources. Others were escaping religious persecution or other problems. They had brought European culture to the wilds of North America, but America would never be Europe. Simply the act of leaving their countries and making the dangerous voyage across the Atlantic Ocean changed the colonists. They came from different countries with widely differing backgrounds, but their journey was something all the immigrants had in common.

Carving out a home in North America was hard work as well. People needed courage and independence to survive. The land they had come to shaped their character and changed them nearly as much as they changed it by their presence and the cultures they brought with them.

House of Parliment

Although the colonists still considered themselves British, they were becoming Americans. To survive, they developed traits and skills Europe had not demanded of them. England's king had their loyalty, but they enjoyed the fact that thousands of miles separated them from England and they could generally govern themselves.

Though American colonists might have believed they deserved the same rights as British citizens back home, Parliament did not see things the same way. Britain had planted colonies all across the world to make money. The colonies might be a part of the British

Seven Years War

Fought in Europe, North America, and India, the Seven Years War (1756–1763) was the first "world war." The long war was fought with France, Austria, Russia, Saxony, Sweden, and Spain (after 1762) on one side and Prussia, Great Britain, and Hanover on the other. The main conflict centered around two points: the colonial rivalry between France and Great Britain, and the struggle between Austria and Prussia for control of Germany. Fighting began in the Ohio River area in 1754, and then spread to Europe.

The conflict between the British and French ended with the Treaty of Paris. Britain gained lots of land and influence at the expense of the French. France was given the choice of keeping her land in America or her islands in the Caribbean. France chose the sugar-rich islands, giving the land west of the Mississippi River to Great Britain. Spain lost Florida to Great Britain, but took New Orleans and the Louisiana Territory west of the Mississippi River from the French.

Empire, but they existed for Britain's benefit. The Seven Years War had left Britain with the world's largest national debt. Looking for ways to pay the debt, George Grenville, British Prime Minister and Chancellor of the Exchequer, suggested Parliament impose a stamp tax on the American colonies. After all, half the debt came from the North American part of the war. In addition, the British already had a stamp tax at home and the colonists paid much less in taxes to the king each year than did citizens in Britain. A stamp tax for the American colonists seemed only logical to Grenville and the members of Parliament.

That is not how the colonists saw the situation. True, they paid less tax directly to Britain

British soldiers during the Seven Years War

13

than did those who lived there, but they paid taxes to their local governments as well, which evened things out. In fact, the colonists paid much higher prices than people in England did—five time as much for some documents.

The Stamp Act was set to take effect on November 1, 1765. By mid-August, the indignation of the colonists gave way to public demonstrations. On August 14, the people of Boston discovered an **effigy** of the recently appointed Boston stamp master, Andrew Oliver, hanging from a large elm tree on the edge of town.

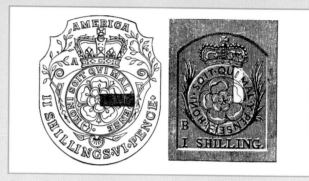

Facsimiles of the British stamps

Reenactment of American colonists gathering in a tavern

Throughout the day, crowds gathered under the straw figure, yelling and shaking their fists at it. At sunset, the mob cut down the effigy and carried it through the streets, shouting, "Liberty, property, and no stamps!" They stopped at the new stamp office to tear down the unfinished building and burn it, then marched on to Oliver's home. Men pounded on the door and shouted for Oliver to come out, but the house remained dark and silent. The stamp master, seeing the mood of the people, had left earlier in the day. When no one answered their shouts, someone in the crowd threw a rock. A window shattered. Soon, all the windows in the house had been smashed. By the time the mob dispersed, they had trampled Oliver's garden into ruin, ripped down the trees in his yard, and

A Stamp Act official being attacked and beaten

*An **effigy** is a crude figure made to look like a hated person.*

A Stamp Act effigy

stampeded through his house, breaking up most of the furniture. The next day, fearing for his life, Oliver resigned his commission as stamp master.

Parliament had appointed local colonists as stamp masters, thinking the people would accept them more easily than men sent over from Britain. Instead, the colonists furiously denounced the new stamp masters as traitors. All over the American colonies stamp masters resigned rather than face the anger of their neighbors.

Delegates *are people chosen to represent other people.*

Repeal *means to revoke by legislative action.*

In October, **delegates** from nine of the thirteen colonies met in New York City to discuss the Stamp Act. Over the next three weeks, the members of the Stamp Act Congress drafted a Declaration of Rights to send to the king and Parliament, asking for a **repeal** of the Stamp Act. In the declaration, they asserted their loyalty to the king and Britain and claimed equal rights with other Englishmen. These rights included, the declaration stated, not being taxed without their consent or the consent of their representatives. The colonies had no voting representatives in Parliament,

Colonial Williamsburg

so, they claimed, the stamp tax was not constitutionally legal.

On November 1, the Stamp Act went into effect. Church bells up and down the coast of North America tolled mournfully for the death of freedom, and flags flew at half-staff. No stamps were sold. Almost all the stamp masters had resigned, and the stamps themselves were destroyed or locked up on British ships in the harbors. No business could be done since nearly everything now required a stamp. Women spun their own yarn and wove their own cloth rather than buy imported British cloth.

Bostonians in distress

Colonial women spun their own yarn and wove fabrics (reenactment).

When Parliament met in December, they realized they had lost. All trade with the American colonies had stopped on November 1, and Britain desperately needed the money that business with the colonists brought in. Parliament was unhappy about repealing the tax, but pressure from British merchants finally convinced them. On March 17, 1766, Parliament repealed the Stamp Act. The next day, Parliament defiantly passed the Declaratory Act, stating that they had the power to make laws concerning

An engraving by Paul Revere shows Britist ships occupying Boston's harbor.

the American colonies in all cases. The colonists, thrilled with their success at getting the Stamp Act repealed, ignored the Declaratory Act.

A year later, Parliament passed the Townshend Acts, raising the tax on common goods such as glass, paper, paint, and tea. Again, the colonists reacted with outrage to the new taxes. They had just won the battle over the Stamp Act, but now Parliament was again ignoring their right of "no taxation without representation."

Once more, the colonists stopped buying the newly taxed goods from the British. They made their own paper, stopped painting their houses, and bought tea smuggled down from Canada. In 1770, Parliament repealed all the taxes except the tax on tea. The colonists had found the tea tax the most insulting. Nearly everyone drank tea, and they did not do without it happily. Tensions rose even higher.

On the evening of March 5, 1770, a group of young men in Boston started throwing snowballs, chunks of ice, and pieces of garbage at the British sentry posted in front of the Customs House. As the mob grew larger, the sentry called

The Boston Massacre

for help, and Captain Thomas Preston arrived with eight or nine soldiers. The crowd pressed closer, shouting and jeering. The participants of the riot never completely agreed on what happened next, but under some degree of provocation, several British soldiers fired into the crowd. Afterward, five men lay dead and six more seriously wounded. Captain Preston later stood trial for murder, but was acquitted through the efforts of his lawyer, John Adams.

The clash between a mob of Boston townsmen and several British soldiers was hardly a true massacre. The ***activist*** Samuel Adams first began calling the event the Boston Massacre in an attempt to keep the people's anger high. Silversmith Paul Revere added to the ***propaganda*** with an engraving of the event. The engraving showed a group of organized British soldiers firing together into a crowd of civilians milling around harmlessly.

Despite the efforts of Samuel Adams and Paul Revere, tensions in the American colonies eased. People got used to ***boycotting*** tea shipped in by British trading companies and drinking smuggled tea. Life went back to normal.

But by 1773, the British East India Company, which had been importing 320,000 pounds of tea a year to the colonies, could only sell about 520 pounds of tea a year. The company's warehouse overflowed with tea, and bankruptcy seemed the only option. In May of 1773, Parliament stepped in to help the company by passing the Tea Act. The Tea Act gave the British East India Company a *monopoly* on tea, eliminating competing British companies. The act also drastically reduced the tea tax. This meant the British East India Company could sell their tea at cheaper prices than the smugglers charged.

The Tea Act annoyed the colonists. Even though they could now buy tea more cheaply, they felt Parliament was trying to force them to accept paying the tax. When the British East India Company's ships arrived filled with tea, the colonists in New York and Philadelphia refused to let them dock. In other harbors, the ships docked, but colonists immediately unloaded the tea into warehouses and locked it up to rot. Boston, however, allowed three ships to dock as usual.

On the morning of December 16, 1773, thousands of men from Boston and the surrounding villages crowded into the Old South Meeting House to hear Samuel Adams' fiery condemnation of the Tea Act. Angry townspeople had prevented the tea from being unloaded from the ships waiting in the Boston harbor. Now they wanted the tea ships to leave without any taxes being paid. Samuel Adams quickly organized a group to take their demands to the Collector of Customs.

From the Meeting House, the men marched to the Custom House to insist the ships be sent away. The Collector of Customs refused. The governor had ordered the ships to stay until the tea was unloaded and the taxes paid.

An **activist** is someone who acts in support of a cause.

Propaganda is ideas or facts spread deliberately to further a cause or to damage another's cause.

Boycotting means refusing to buy or use a specific product.

A **monopoly** is the exclusive ownership of or the right to sell a commodity.

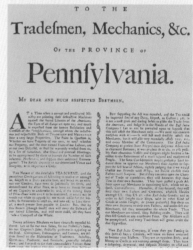

Broadside against the East India Company, 1773

Chaos is a state of extreme disorganized behavior.

The group returned to the Meeting House, where the crowd waited to hear whether their demands had been met. "This meeting can do no more to save the country," Samuel Adams said, after they announced the failure of their mission. The building was silent for one long second. Suddenly, a man dressed as an Indian and covered with war paint stood in the balcony and whooped. "Griffin's Wharf!" another man shouted, jumping to his feet.

The meeting broke up in *chaos*. People streamed from the building, rushing through the cold winter night down to the harbor. Several dozen men dressed to look like Mohawk Indians led the way, shouting war cries. Once at Griffin's Wharf, about sixty of the men boarded the ships while others kept watch nearby. For the next three hours, the men dumped crate after crate of tea into the Boston harbor—342 crates in all. Those who stood by watched silently as thousands of dollars worth of tea slowly filled the waters of the harbor.

The British reacted in outrage at the destruction of private property—the tea—caused by the Boston Tea Party. Parliament immediately passed a series of acts, which they called

Samuel Adams

The Boston Tea Party

23

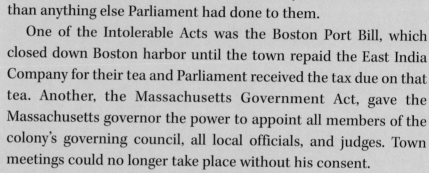

Intolerable means unbearable; unable to be tolerated.

the Coercive or Punitive Acts, because they intended them to punish the colonists and bring them back under control. The colonists called them the *Intolerable* Acts because they were more offensive than anything else Parliament had done to them.

One of the Intolerable Acts was the Boston Port Bill, which closed down Boston harbor until the town repaid the East India Company for their tea and Parliament received the tax due on that tea. Another, the Massachusetts Government Act, gave the Massachusetts governor the power to appoint all members of the colony's governing council, all local officials, and judges. Town meetings could no longer take place without his consent.

Parliament did not foresee the greatest effect of the Intolerable Acts: The injustice of the acts brought the colonies closer together. Boston could not function without its port, so the other colonies showed their support by sending food supplies to help the Bostonians out.

In September of 1774, fifty-five delegates met in Philadelphia's Carpenter's Hall to discuss what actions the colonies should take next. Many delegates held prominent social positions in their own communities, but most had never met each other until now. Delegates built strong friendships at this First Continental Congress that would last through the war to come and the building of the new country.

The delegates of the First Continental Congress debated and discussed for nearly two months. In the end, they had created the Association, which called on the colonies to completely stop using and importing British goods. They had adopted the Suffolk Resolves, giving Massachusetts the right to form its own govern-

King George III

The Boston Tea Party

ment and become a free state until Parliament revoked the Intolerable Acts. Finally, they had drafted the Declaration of Rights and Grievances, addressed to King George III. If the situation in the American colonies had not improved by the next spring, the Congress would meet again in May.

Most of the delegates, as well as most of the colonists, even now still considered themselves loyal subjects of the king. Their complaints were against Parliament, not the king. Hardly anyone even thought of independence from Britain. They simply wanted things to go back to the way they had been in the early 1760s, before the Stamp Act. As they saw it, if Parliament would just give them a say in the creation of the laws that governed them, everyone would be happy.

The struggle for no taxation without representation had started to get out of hand, though. Every time the colonists resisted Parliament's unfair taxes, Parliament struck back with even harsher laws, such as the Intolerable Acts. Though the colonists wanted to stay loyal to Britain, some could see the possibility that the future might hold a difficult choice: either pay the hated taxes, or separate and become an independent nation.

The Intolerable Acts

- The Boston Port Act—Closed the port of Boston until the British East India Company received payment for the tea destroyed by the colonists and Britain received the taxes due on that same tea.

- The Massachusetts Government Act—Gave the governor the power to appoint all governing officials and judges, instead of letting the colonists elect them. Also required the colonists to get written permission from the governor before holding any kind of town meeting.

- The Administration of Justice Act—Gave British officials who had been accused of a crime the right to be tried in England or in another colony in order to receive a fair trial.

- The Quartering Act—Required the colonists to feed and house British soldiers, in their own homes if necessary.

- The Quebec Act—Provided Canadian Catholics with religious freedom and extended Quebec's borders to include large territories already claimed by the American colonists. The British hoped the Quebec Act would win the support of Canadians.

Carpenter's Hall, site of the First Continental Congress

Paul Revere statue in front of Boston's North Church

Two
TAKING A STAND FOR INDEPENDENCE

Hooves pounded along the moonlit road in the Massachusetts countryside just north of Boston. Paul Revere leaned low over his horse's neck, his eyes scanning the road ahead for any sign of British Redcoats. They had almost caught him once, several miles back, and he had needed to take a detour away from the main road to avoid them.

A farmhouse caught his eye, and he turned his horse to gallop up to the front door. Without dismounting, he pounded on the door. "The regulars are coming!" he shouted. "The Redcoats are headed for Concord!" When the farmer called back, Revere kicked his horse into motion and rode on toward Lexington. He still had to warn Samuel Adams and John Hancock before the British reached them.

The Massachusetts patriots had known for days that General Gage and his troops planned to crush the growing rebellion in the area. On April 18, 1775, they watched every movement the British soldiers made. In the evening, they learned Gage and his men would march that night to destroy the colony's cannon and weapon supplies in Concord and to arrest

***Treason** is the offense of trying to overthrow the government; it is the only crime specifically mentioned in the U.S. Constitution.*

*A **militia** is a group of citizens organized for military service.*

Samuel Adams and John Hancock for ***treason***. Immediately, Paul Revere left to warn the men and rouse the countryside.

Massachusetts colonists had prepared for such an event for months. The ***militia*** members called themselves Minutemen, because they could be ready to fight with only a minute's notice. As Paul Revere spread the word, farmers threw on clothes, grabbed their muskets, and hurried to join the other Minutemen in Lexington and Concord.

When the British troops, led by Major Pitcairn, reached Lexington at sunrise, they found almost seventy local Minutemen,

Paul Revere's ride

standing shoulder to shoulder, blocking their passage through town. "Out of the way!" Major Pitcairn shouted, but the patriots refused to move. Several British soldiers fired shots in the air, hoping to scatter the men blocking the road, but nothing happened. The Minutemen kept their muskets ready at their sides, but did not make any moves to attack. They had been ordered not to fire unless the British actually shot at them.

Finally, Major Pitcairn lost his patience. Pulling out his pistol, he fired into the crowd of men. "Fire!" he shouted to his men. Several patriots fell dead or wounded, but now they fought back. The first shot fired that morning became known as "the shot heard round the world." This first armed resistance against the British marked the beginning of the Revolutionary War for America's independence.

The British soldiers outnumbered the Minutemen by several hundred, however, and this opening battle ended quickly. Eight of the local militia had been killed, while no British soldiers at all died.

Encouraged by their easy victory, the Redcoats cheered as they marched north toward Concord. They anticipated another quick

A statue of a Minuteman stands in Boston

31

Liberty Poles

In Boston, before the Revolutionary War, patriots calling themselves the Sons of Liberty gathered under a large elm tree to hold their meetings. The tree soon became known as the Liberty Tree. Towns in the area without large trees in their town squares put up wooden poles called Liberty Poles to show their support for the patriots. Red-and-white striped Liberty Flags flew from the tops of these poles. When the British entered the towns, often one of the first things they did was chop down the Liberty Pole.

Battle of Lexington

battle to put the colonists in their place, and then they could go home for the day. April 19 was already warm and humid—by noon the temperatures would reach 85 degrees Fahrenheit (almost 30 degrees Celsius) in the shade—and no one wanted to spend more time than necessary controlling rebellious colonists.

When the British arrived in Concord, they found no resisting force waiting. They had heard rumors of the whole countryside taking up arms against them, but now they thought the rumors were exaggerated. No one in Concord appeared to have any intention of fighting them.

The Minutemen had not deserted Concord, however. They had gathered on a nearby hilltop, where they had moved the cannon and most of the weapon stores for safekeeping. From the hill, they watched as the Redcoats entered town.

With no resistance, the British soldiers wandered through the town, looting and destroying. Leaving men to guard the roads in and out of Concord, the soldiers destroyed the supplies the patriots had left in town. They cut down the Liberty Pole and burned the courthouse.

Battle at Concord's North Bridge

While the British troops destroyed parts of Concord, more colonists arrived to join the patriots north of town. Finally, late in the morning, the men attacked the two hundred Redcoats at the North Bridge. Shooting at each other across the river, not many were injured, but as more colonists kept arriving, the British realized they had underestimated the patriots. Major Pitcairn called a retreat, and the colonists followed. All the British soldiers might eventually have been

killed that day, but at Lexington they met a group of twelve hundred British reinforcements. The British spent the rest of the day fighting their way back to Boston. When night fell, the colonists had lost 95 men, the British 273.

After the battles of Lexington and Concord, the patriots put Boston under siege. The city could still receive supplies through the harbor, but the rebels made sure no British soldiers could get in or out on the roads. For nearly two months, the militia camped at Cambridge, across the Charles River from Boston. Finally,

they heard that General Gage planned an attack on their forces to fight his way out of the city. On the night of June 16, 1775, patriot general Israel Putnam and hundreds of his men built fortifications in the side of Breed's Hill. Originally, Putnam had been ordered to build the defenses on nearby Bunker Hill, but Breed's Hill appeared easier to defend.

In the morning, when the British woke up and saw the new trenches on Breed's Hill, they organized an attack. After three assaults on the rebel fortifications, the British finally won the

Reenactment of Redcoats in battle

35

Monument on Bunker Hill

battle, taking Breed's Hill. The victory was costly, however; over a thousand British soldiers had been killed or wounded—nearly half their troops. Despite the fact that the battle took place at Breed's Hill, it became famous as the Battle of Bunker Hill.

Although the British had won the battle, their difficult victory and heavy losses affected both sides. The British realized now that the colonists would not be easily crushed. General Thomas Gage, who commanded the British forces in America, returned to England shortly after the Battle of Bunker Hill. In his report to Parliament, he told them, "a large army must at length be employed to reduce these people," and recommended hiring foreign troops to help with the effort. Parliament followed his suggestion and hired Hessians from Germany to help fight the Americans.

The colonists, on the other hand, saw that the British forces were not invincible after all. The British had been the superior force. They had outnumbered the patriots nearly two to one. They had been trained soldiers, while the patriots were farmers and shopkeepers. The Battle of Bunker Hill proved the colonists had a chance of succeeding in their fight.

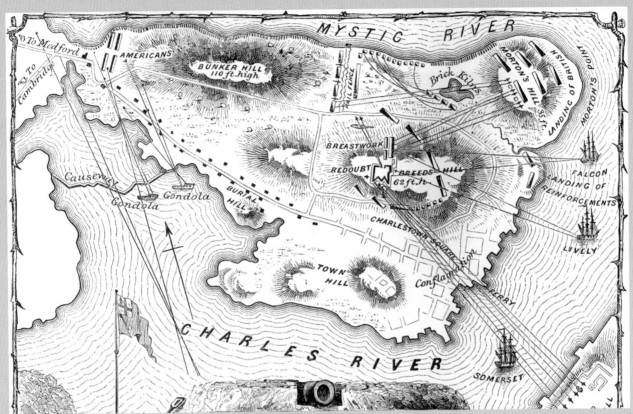

Map of the action at Breed's Hill

On May 10, 1775, a month before the Battle of Bunker Hill, the Second Continental Congress had convened in Philadelphia. Alarmed at the events taking place around Boston, they immediately called for the creation of a Continental Army. On June 15, Congress elected George Washington to serve as commander in chief of the new army. Washington agreed to take the position, but only if he could serve without pay; only his expenses would be paid. Two weeks

The Battle of Bunker Hill

later, Washington arrived outside of Boston to take command of the rebel troops.

Although the Revolutionary War was now truly under way, the colonists *still* thought of themselves as part of Britain, loyal to King George. They fought British soldiers because they wanted to show Parliament they could not be intimidated. Parliament needed to respect their position and give them representation in matters that concerned them.

In January of 1776, Thomas Paine, a British political writer living in Philadelphia, published a pamphlet called *Common Sense*. In the pamphlet, Paine recommended that the American colonies immediately declare their independence from Britain and become a new nation. Paine argued that America was not British since people from many different European nations had settled here. Also, he argued, if Britain truly was the "mother country" of the American colonies, its behavior was even worse: "But Britain is the parent country, say some. Then the more shame upon her conduct. Even brutes do not devour their young, nor savages make war upon their families."

Common Sense electrified the American colonists. Nearly every **literate** person in the colonies read the little book. More than anything, *Common Sense* forced the colonists to examine their true views on the conflict with Britain. Some found Paine's words expressed their growing feelings on the matter; others worried that his extreme views would have a negative effect.

Colonists found themselves beginning to divide into groups of Loyalists and Patriots. Loyalists remained loyal to Britain through-

Literate means able to read and write.

Thomas Paine

out the war. Many Loyalists found life under British rule comfortable and satisfying. Others felt they had something to lose if America became an independent country. These included African Americans who had been promised freedom if they fought for the British, and Native Americans who believed they would have more rights under British rule. After the war, thousands of Loyalists returned to Britain or moved north to Canada.

As people continued to read *Common Sense*, the idea that Congress should draft a declaration of their independence from Britain started to take root. On June 7, 1776, Richard Henry Lee, one of the representatives from Virginia in the Continental Congress, proposed "that these united colonies are and of right ought to be free and independent States." Congress did not immediately agree to the proposal, but they did appoint a committee to write a declaration of independence, in case they should decide to act on it.

Thomas Jefferson wrote most of the Declaration of Independence, while the other committee members—Benjamin Franklin, John Adams, Roger Sherman, and Robert Livingston—helped to edit the document and made suggestions about its content. On June 28 the committee presented the Declaration of Independence to the Continental Congress. Over the next several days, Congress debated the Declaration, arguing about changes various members felt should be made. The largest change removed a passage

Independence Hall

41

in which Jefferson attacked the slave trade. On July 4, 1776, Congress approved the Declaration of Independence. This date would forever be known as Independence Day in the United States.

In the months after the Continental Congress declared America an independent nation, fighting raged throughout the Northeast. In 1777, General Burgoyne led ten thousand British soldiers down from Canada, intending to take over Albany, New York. The British planned to separate New England from the southern colonies by taking control of the Hudson River. This would divide the colonies in

Trumbull's mural of the signing of the Declaration of Independence

The Spirit of Independence

They pushed south until Patriot forces stopped them just east of the town of Saratoga, in the Hudson River Valley.

On September 19, the British marched to try to take Saratoga. They had not gone far when they encountered the Americans. After a day of

General Burgoyne

half, separating their strength and making it harder for them to fight back.

During late spring, General Burgoyne moved down along Lake Champlain, and the British re-took the forts at Crown Point and Ticonderoga they had lost to the Americans two years earlier.

fighting, and heavy losses on the British side, General Burgoyne succeeded in capturing Freeman's Farm, which he then used as a base.

On October 7, running low on supplies, General Burgoyne and his tired, miserable army again tried to take Saratoga. When the British moved west, the Americans attacked. Another hard day of fighting finally drove the British back to the fortifications they had dug out in Freeman's Farm. The next day, Burgoyne and his

The British surrender after the Battle of Saratoga

men started to retreat north but ran into American forces. Finally, on October 17, General Burgoyne surrendered. He had lost a thousand men, his supplies had dwindled to nearly nothing, and his expected reinforcements had never arrived. The American troops, on the other hand, had plenty of supplies and their numbers grew constantly. The Americans had suffered just under five hundred casualties in the Battle of Saratoga, and ended with nearly twenty thousand healthy troops.

Allied means joined to help each other.

The Americans' decisive victory at the Battle of Saratoga caught the attention of the world. Suddenly, the American colonists were not simply a small wilderness force pestering the well-trained British. Instead, they had become an effective army worth noticing.

After the Battle of Saratoga, the British offered to let the American colonies rule themselves from within the British Empire. Even five years earlier, this would have been a great victory, but the colonists had come too far to stop now at anything short of independence.

The British offer made the French nervous, though. Now that America had developed a capable fighting force, if they *allied* themselves with the British again they might attack French colonies in the New World, like the French West Indies. Rather than allow America to join the British against them, France offered an alliance of its own. France's help after the Franco-American Treaty of 1778 greatly aided the American forces.

George Washington at Valley Forge

During the winter of 1777–1778, General George Washington and the Continental Army camped at Valley Forge, Pennsylvania. That winter the American army faced some of its most difficult moments. From the start, the men were starving, with ragged, tattered clothes and worn-out boots. As the winter crawled on, conditions deteriorated. The army suffered from cold, hunger, and disease. As many as three thousand men died at Valley Forge in the six months Washington and the Continental Army spent there.

News of America's alliance with France came to Valley Forge in February and offered great encouragement to General Washington and his troops. Then, as spring arrived, conditions began to improve steadily. Supplies started to arrive regularly, and new officers came to help maintain the camp. By the time the army marched away from Valley Forge in June, they had been transformed from rag-tag, starving men into an organized, confident army.

During 1778 and 1779, the British started shifting their focus away from the northern colonies and toward the South. The British felt the population of the South was more sympathetic to their cause and therefore more likely to support them. The British, under General Cornwallis, quickly captured Georgia and much of South Carolina. By 1781, British troops had pushed through North Carolina and as far north as Fredericksburg, Virginia.

In the summer of 1781, Washington moved troops toward New York City in an effort to make the British think the city was the next major American target. Men took up posts at forts in the area to keep up the illusion. Then, Washington and the

French general Rochambeau moved quickly south toward General Cornwallis and the British at Yorktown, Virginia. Meanwhile, a French fleet, commanded by Admiral de Grasse, attacked the British ships in the Chesapeake Bay and took control over the bay.

On September 28, the combined American and French land forces reached Yorktown and circled to surround the British. The battle raged for nearly a month. The British were severely outnumbered. By the time the other British generals in New York City decided to send help, Cornwallis and his men had run out of time. On October 17, General Cornwallis finally agreed to surrender,

Battle of Yorktown

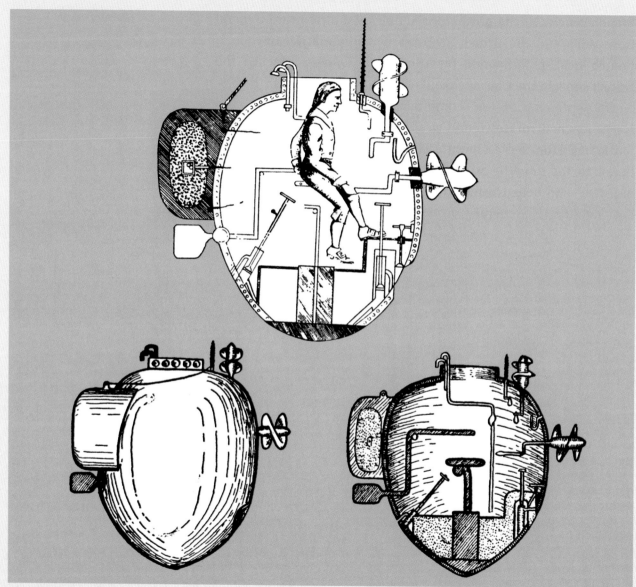

The Turtle—the world's first combat submarine

The *Turtle*

The world's first combat submarine was used during the Revolutionary War. The *Turtle* was built by David Bushnell of Connecticut, and it contained only enough air to support life for half an hour. A bottle of phosphorus was used to illuminate the compass and the water gauge, and water was let into the bottom to submerge the little submarine, then pumped out for surfacing.

On September 6, 1776, the *Turtle* approached the flagship of the British fleet and tried to fasten a bomb to her hull. The copper-sheathed H.M.S. *Eagle* was too tough, however, for the bomb to be attached properly. The explosion hurt neither the *Turtle* nor the *Eagle*—but it did give British Admiral Howe a substantial scare.

although, claiming to be sick, he did not personally attend the surrender ceremonies.

The Battle of Yorktown was the last serious battle of the Revolutionary War. As soon as news of Cornwallis's surrender reached Britain, the Prime Minister, Lord North, resigned from office. In April 1782, Parliament decided not to continue the war in North America. Over the next year, British troops left America and traveled back to Britain.

Surrender of Cornwallis

The Treaty of Paris. The painting is unfinished because only the Americans agreed to sit for the portrait painter; the British did not care to be included in the painting

BE IT REMEMBERED!

THAT on the 17th of October, 1781, Lieutenant-General Earl CORNWALLIS, with above Five thousand British Troops, surrendered themselves Prisoners of War to his Excellency Gen. GEORGE WASHINGTON, Commander in Chief of the allied Forces of France and America.

LAUS DEO!

Confiscated means taken away by the government.

Southern Middle Media
5235 Solomon's Island Rd.
Lothian, MD 20711

Britain and the new nation of the United States of America signed the final peace treaty ending the Revolutionary War on September 3, 1783. The treaty negotiations took place in Paris, with Benjamin Franklin, John Adams, and John Jay signing the Treaty of Paris on behalf of the United States. By the terms of the treaty, Britain recognized the independence of the United States, and the Americans agreed not to persecute any Loyalists remaining in the country, to give back *confiscated* Loyalist property, and to allow the British to collect debts owned them by the Americans.

The American Revolution began with unhappiness over the unfair taxes Parliament imposed on its colonists. In the beginning, the American colonists had no intention of breaking away from their mother country. Life under British rule became increasingly unbearable, however, until the colonists were ready to declare their independence and fight for freedom. After more than six years of fighting, Americans had gained their independence, and the United States existed as a new nation. Now, American leaders faced the enormous task of shaping their new country.

GLORIOUS NEWS.

PROVIDECE, October 25, 1781.

Three o'Clock, P. M.

THIS MOMENT an EXPRESS arrived at his Honour the Deputy-Governor's, from Col. Christopher Olney, Commandant on Rhode-Island, announcing the important Intelligence of the Surrender of Lord Cornwallis and his Army, an Account of which was printed This Morning at Newport, and is as follows, viz.

Newport, October 25, 1781.

YESTERDAY afternoon arrived in this Harbour Capt. Lovett, of the Schooner Adventure, from York-River, in Chesapeak-Bay (which he left the 20th Instant) and brought us the glorious News of the Surrender of Lord CORNWALLIS and his Army Prisoners of War to the allied Army, under the Command of our illustrious General, and the French Fleet, under the Command of his Excellency the Count de GRASSE.

A Cessation of Arms took Place on Thursday the 18th Instant, in Consequence of Proposals from Lord Cornwallis for a Capitulation. His Lordship proposed a Cessation of Twenty-four Hours, but Two only were granted by His Excellency General WASHINGTON. The Articles were completed the same Day, and the next Day the allied Army took Possession of York-Town.

By this glorious Conquest, NINE THOUSAND of the Enemy, including Seamen, fell into our Hands, with an immense Quantity of Warlike Stores, a forty Gun Ship, a Frigate, an armed Vessel, and about One Hundred Sail of Transports.

A broadside announcing the British defeat at Yorktown

First flag at Independence Hall, Philadelphia

Three
CREATING A REPUBLIC

Image you and a group of your friends had the job of deciding which rules would govern your school. Would you let individual classrooms decide on some of their own rules? Do you think you and your friends would have trouble agreeing how to run the school? No matter how much time you spent going over the policies, situations would probably come up that you hadn't anticipated.

The Founding Fathers of the United States of America faced these problems on a much larger scale. At the same time as the Continental Congress assigned Thomas Jefferson to write the Declaration of Independence in 1776, they also *commissioned* John Dickinson, a representative from Pennsylvania, to write a document laying out how the new country would be governed.

Eight days after Congress voted to accept the Declaration of Independence, Dickinson presented them with the Articles of Confederation. Dickinson was very *conservative* and, in fact, had argued against accepting the Declaration of Independence. His version of the Articles of Confederation would create a strong central government uniting the individual states. Most of the other

Commissioned means hired to perform a task.

Conservative means against change, preferring to keep things the way they are.

53

congressional delegates did not like the idea of giving too much power to a central government. They feared such a government might start oppressing the American people, like Britain had done.

Congress's concerns about certain points in Dickinson's version of the Articles of Confederation meant

they did not accept them right away. Instead, they discussed the articles on and off over the next year, making changes and then discussing those changes. Finally, on November 15, 1777, the Continental Congress voted to accept a revised version of the Articles of Confederation.

Colonial currency

54

DELAWARE.

PENNSYLVANIA.

NEW JERSEY.

GEORGIA.

[He who transplanted still sustains.]

CONNECTICUT.

[By the sword he seeks peace under Liberty.]

MASSACHUSETTS.

MARYLAND.

SOUTH CAROLINA

[Thus always with tyrants.]

VIRGINIA.

[More Elevated.]

NEW YORK.

NEW HAMPSHIRE.

NORTH CAROLINA.

RHODE ISLAND.

The seals for the individual states

The Articles of Confederation gave the individual states a lot of freedom to govern themselves. The states united in "a firm league of friendship," but the central government tying them together was weak. The central government consisted of Congress, made up of delegates from each state.

Under the articles, Congress had the power to declare war, make **treaties**, keep up an army and navy, and make money. However, to accomplish any of these things, Congress needed at least nine out of the thirteen states to agree. To revise the articles, all the states had to agree.

Treaties are agreements reached through negotiations between governing bodies.

Early American coins

57

Radical means extreme.

*An **ordinance** is a law.*

Unincorporated means not united into a formal structure, such as a town.

Surveyed means to have measured an area, determining its exact size.

Patriot soldier (reenactment)

Only the individual states had the power to tax the people. Therefore, Congress had no way of raising money to meet its own expenses. In addition, even though Congress could make certain laws, nothing prevented the states from ignoring those laws and doing whatever they liked.

As soon as America declared its independence, Congress encouraged each state to write its own constitution. Some states revised their current colonial charters, while others wrote entirely new documents. In the same way, some states made very few changes to the existing laws and government, while others made **radical** changes. Pennsylvania, for example, granted every male taxpayer and his sons the right to vote, something only landowners were often granted.

The Founding Fathers intended the individual states to carry the strength of the Union. The colonies had united to free themselves from the British, and while the Revolutionary War raged, this cause was enough to bind them together. Once the war ended, however, problems with the Articles of Confederation began to surface.

The war had started because of friction over excessive taxes. To make sure the United States did not do the same thing as Britain, Congress had no power to tax the people. Congress needed money, however, so the delegates agreed that each state would give money toward the running of the national government. This seemed like a good idea at first, but the states had their own problems and expenses. Congress received only a quarter of the agreed-on amount from the states.

Articles of Confederation (1777)

The Articles of Confederation made sure to give individual states more authority than a central government. These are the first three articles:

I.   The Stile of this Confederacy shall be "The United States of America."

II.   Each state retains its sovereignty, freedom, and independence, and every power, jurisdiction, and right, which is not by this Confederation expressly delegated to the United States, in Congress assembled.

III.   The said States hereby severally enter into a firm league of friendship with each other, for their common defense, the security of their liberties, and their mutual and general welfare, binding themselves to assist each other, against all force offered to, or attacks made upon them, or any of them, on account of religion, sovereignty, trade, or any other pretense whatever.

One way Congress found to raise its own money came from the land to the west of the existing states. By the terms of the Treaty of Paris, the United States owned all the land east of the Mississippi, but most of that area consisted of untamed wilderness at this time. On May 20, 1785, Congress approved the Land Ordinance of 1785. This **ordinance** described how the **unincorporated** land would be divided. First, the land would be **surveyed**. Next, it would be divided into townships six miles square. Each township would have thirty-six sections of one mile square. The sixteenth section of each township would be set aside for a public school and each of the other sections sold for a minimum of a dollar an acre ($640). Congress would receive the money from these sales.

In 1787, Congress adopted the Northwest Ordinance, which set out how new states would join the Union. This gave further organization to the western territories. Until a territory's population reached five thousand, Congress would appoint its governors. After that, the territory could elect its own legislature and send delegates to Congress, although these delegates could not vote. When the population reached sixty thousand, the territorial legislature could write a state constitution and submit it to Congress. After Congress approved the constitution, the new state would enter the Union.

The Northwest Ordinance gave new states entering the Union the same status as already existing states. Most nations kept their new lands inferior to themselves, such as Britain had

Farmer's plow

Colonial farmer (reenactment)

done with its American colonies. Granting equality to new states was a radical concept. This principle encouraged westward expansion, since Americans knew they would have the same rights wherever they lived in the country.

In spite of the efforts of Congress to raise money, economic problems in America in-creased. British companies wanted to collect debts the colonies had owed them before the war. The Treaty of Paris had given Britain that right, but American states did not have enough money. To pay the British, many states began heavily taxing their residents, who also had very little money. Some farmers lost everything and were forced to sell their lands and possessions to pay their debts. Others even found themselves in debtors' prison.

The high taxes seemed horribly unfair to Americans. Many of the New England farmers threatened with imprisonment had fought in

Daniel Shays' rebellion

the war of independence and returned home with almost nothing to show for it. Congress did not have the funds to give them their full earnings, since Congress had little money of its own.

By 1786, some farmers had lost patience with the system. Mobs marched on debtors' courts to keep them from meeting. Daniel Shays, a thirty-nine-year-old captain who had served in the Revolutionary War, led the rebellious farmers. Soon, the rebels began calling themselves "Shays' men." Shays and those who followed him did not think of themselves as doing anything wrong. They fought now for freedom, just as they had done against the British. They did not expect the Massachusetts government would raise an army to defeat them. They believed their actions would change the unfair practice of heavy taxation.

The Massachusetts governor, James Bowdoin, did not see the Shays rebellion as a fair and ***democratic*** means of problem solving. Alarmed at the chaos erupting in the countryside, Bowdoin and other Massachusetts leaders used their own money to fund a private army to put down the uprising.

In January of 1787, Shays and a group of two thousand men—now completely enraged at the lack of results their efforts had produced—attacked the **armory** in Springfield, Massachusetts. The Shays men intended to seize the weapons and defend themselves against Bowdoin's hastily gathered militia.

As the rebels marched toward the armory, the defending militia, led by General William Shepard, fired cannons at the approaching mob. The attack shocked the rebels; they had not expected such an immediate and brutal assault, and now four of them lay dead, with another twenty wounded. The farmers scattered, fleeing into the woods. A week later, the militia finally ended the uprising, defeating the rebels at Petersham, Massachusetts. Shays himself escaped to Vermont. The Supreme Court sentenced Shays and thirteen of his men to death on counts of treason, but the new governor, John Hancock, pardoned them the next year.

The Shays Rebellion made it clear to the Continental Congress that the Articles of Confederation needed to be replaced. Congress had been powerless to control the events leading to the rebellion. The uprising showed a definite need for a stronger central government. The Articles of Confederation had too many flaws to simply be amended, however. By 1787, Congress was ready to draft an entirely new constitution.

Democratic means acting in a way that is beneficial to most of the people.

An **armory** is where military equipment is stored.

James Bowdoin

The Springfield armory

The signing of the Constitution

Four
THE CONSTITUTIONAL CONVENTION

Philadelphia's bitterly cold winter had passed, and the wet chill of early spring had given way to sudden heat by the time James Madison arrived in early May 1787. Clouds of blackflies collected over puddled streets, and sweltering humidity made life miserable. The Constitutional Convention was scheduled to begin on May 14, and Madison, eager to get started, had arrived from Virginia eleven days early. He had developed a number of ideas about the new Constitution and how it should be different from the current, flawed Articles of Confederation. To Madison's disappointment, not enough of the delegates had arrived by May 14, and the convention did not get started until May 25.

Before traveling to Philadelphia, Madison and the other Virginia delegates had gone over his notes and come up with a plan. Under the Virginia Plan, the United States would be a republic, with decisions made by representatives elected by the people. The federal government would be divided into sections having separate responsibilities, so no one group held too much power. The central, national government would have power over the individual states.

The Virginia Plan supported the creation of two legislative houses (a bicameral legislature). The people would elect the members of the lower house, and the lower house would elect the members of the upper house. Each state would be represented in both houses by a number of representatives proportionate to their population. In other words, more heavily populated states would have more representatives.

Small states did not like the fact that larger states would have more representation than they did. In response to the Virginia Plan, William Paterson presented the New Jersey Plan. This plan made fewer changes in the way the current Continental Congress was set up. Like the current Congress, each state would have one vote each, no matter the population.

For weeks, ugly debates prevailed in the convention. Neither the small states nor the large ones intended to give in. Finally, Roger Sherman, a delegate from Connecticut, proposed a compromise: One legislative house would be represented by population, as the Virginia Plan suggested, while a second house would give an equal number of votes to each state, as the New Jersey Plan wanted.

For several more weeks, the debates went on, ignoring Sherman's idea. On June 18, Alexander Hamilton added his own idea to the mix. Hamilton's plan gave almost all of the power to a single governor and did away with most of the individual states' power. Although the convention delegates agreed Hamilton's plan had some interesting ideas, it gave far too much power to the central government.

Then, on June 27, Luther Martin, from Maryland, stood and added his support to the compromise suggestion. After that point, the convention began to think about the idea more seriously. On July 16, they voted to approve the plan.

The other great controversy at the Constitutional Convention involved slavery. When determining the population of a state (and therefore

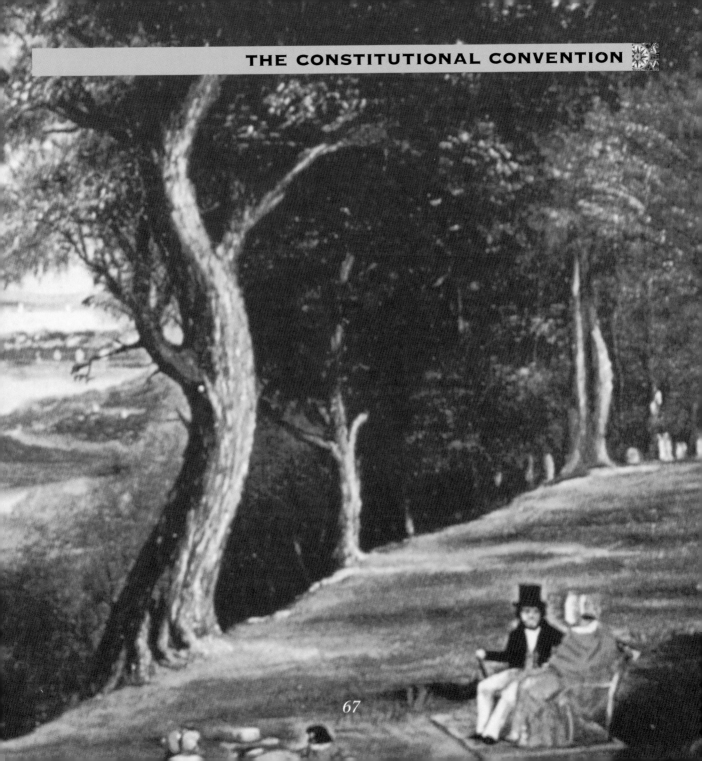

Alexander Hamilton

representatives by importing more slaves. Finally, the delegates agreed to the Three-Fifths Compromise. Each slave would count as three-fifths of a person for the purposes of deciding the number of representatives, but the same number must be used to determine the amount of taxes owed as well.

Debates about whether or not the United

determining the number of representatives in the House of Representatives), the Southern states thought their black slaves should be counted. If slaves were included in the population count, Southern states would increase their numbers of representatives. For this reason, Northern states thought only white people should be counted. Some northerners feared the South would try to increase their number of

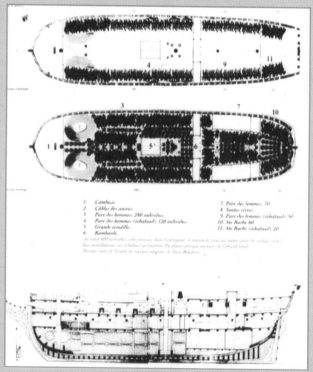

A diagram of a slave ship shows the cramped conditions

States should abolish the slave trade also divided the Constitutional Convention delegates. Though some delegates thought the slave trade was evil, slavery was a way of life in the South. Eventually, the delegates agreed to another compromise. The slave trade could continue for at least another twenty years, and the South would pay taxes on every slave they imported. They could not, however, collect taxes on exported slaves. Under the agreement, the first day the slave trade could possibly be abolished in the United States was on January 1, 1808—and on that day it was abolished.

*A **preamble** is an introductory statement.*

*ized **Posterity** means all future generations.*

__Embodied__ means represented, made real.

At the end of the summer, the debates concluded—although not everyone was satisfied—and the convention appointed a style committee to write the final document. Most of the actual words of the Constitution were written by the brilliant Gouverneur Morris, one of the New York delegates. James Madison later praised Morris's work on the Constitution, saying "a better choice could not have been made" in the selection of who wrote the final document. On September 17, 1787, Morris presented his work to the Convention. His **preamble** read: "We, the people of the United States, in order to form a more perfect union, establish justice, insure domestic tranquillity, provide for the common defense, promote the general welfare, and secure the blessings of liberty to ourselves and our **posterity**, do ordain and establish this Constitution for the United States of America."

The ideas **embodied** in the United States Constitution grew out of the readings, thoughts, and experiences of the Founding Fathers, especially James Madison who drew up much of the

James Madison

Executive has to do with the conduct of public affairs.

Legislative refers to making the laws that govern the country.

Judicial has to do with interpreting the laws legally.

*To **ratify** means to approve formally.*

Constitution's framework. Madison had read widely, including Enlightenment writers such as John Locke and Montesquieu. From these political thinkers, Madison learned the idea of separation of powers, dividing the government into **executive**, **legislative**, and **judicial** branches. This limited abuse of power, since those making the laws did not have the power to carry them out, and another group interpreted their meaning.

Once the convention received the finished copy of the Constitution, the next step called for the individual states to **ratify**

Gouverneur Morris

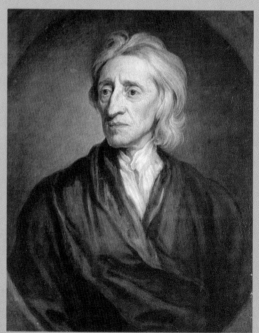

John Locke

The Enlightenment

The Enlightenment was an intellectual movement popular in eighteenth-century Europe. The goal of the movement was to establish a standard for right and wrong, aesthetics (a philosophy dealing with the definition of beauty), and knowledge based on an "enlightened" reality. The movement's leaders, including Immanuel Kant, believed they were leading the world toward progress. The Enlightenment was the framework for the American Revolution and the rise of capitalism.

Some of the common beliefs of Enlightenment thinkers were:

- nations exist to protect the rights of individuals,

- each individual deserves dignity and should be allowed to live with as much personal freedom as possible, including the freedoms of speech and expression, the right to free association, the right to believe (or not to believe) in whatever religion he chooses, and the freedom to elect his own leaders.

- democracy is the best form of government,

- all humanity, all races, ethnicities, nationalities, and religions are equal,

- religious dogma is inferior to logic and philosophy.

it. The earlier Articles of Confederation required all thirteen states to **unanimously** agree, but the delegates of the Constitutional Convention knew that would be impossible; Rhode Island had not even attended the convention. The delegates agreed that when nine states ratified it, the Constitution would become law in those states.

This announcement, coming at the end of the Constitutional Convention, startled the American people. They had thought the convention delegates were revising the Articles of Confederation, not writing an entirely new document. Some worried that the power of their individual states would be threatened by a central government.

In the weeks after the Constitutional Convention, Americans became divided into two groups: the Federalists and the Antifederalists. The Federalists wanted to ratify the new Constitution and liked the idea of a stronger central government. Many of the Federalists had money and owned property. The Antifederalists, on the other hand, wanted to make sure the states kept most of the power and did not want to ratify the Constitution. Antifederalists tended to have less money and property than

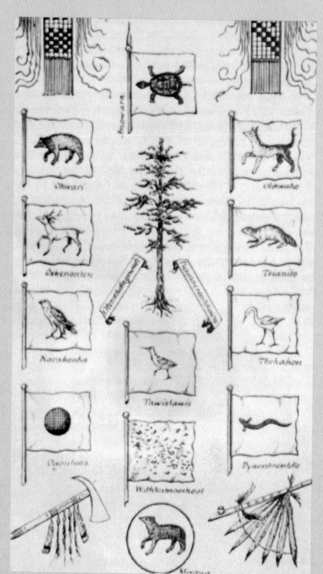

The Iroquois Confederacy

The Iroquois and the Constitution

Today, many people believe the Iroquois League also influenced the Founding Fathers in their development of the Constitution. Similarities do exist between the two documents, although the same could be said of the constitutions of many countries. On October 21, 1988, the United States Senate even passed a resolution stating that the Iroquois Confederacy of Nations had contributed to the development of the United States Constitution. Despite this public acknowledgment, the issue is still very controversial, however, and many scholars consider the connection merely mythical.

Unanimously means done with complete agreement.

the Federalists. They thought the new Constitution was undemocratic and feared a strong central government could too easily oppress the people.

Before 1787 was over, four states—Delaware, Pennsylvania, New Jersey, and Georgia—had already voted to ratify the Constitution. Over the next months, other states continued to add their approval. In June, the ninth state, New Hampshire, voted for ratification. Since enough states had now agreed, the Constitution could become law. As many of the later states added their approval, they asked that a Bill of Rights be drawn up and added to the Constitution. This would protect the states from abuses of power by the federal government.

By the time the new Constitution took effect on March 4, 1789, two more states had ratified it as well. The final two states really had no choice but to ratify, although they still doubted whether this was the right thing to do. Until they agreed to accept the Constitution, they did not truly belong to the United States. On November 21, 1789, North Carolina ratified the Constitution, and finally, on May 29, 1790,

Rhode Island, the last of the thirteen colonies, voted to accept the Constitution as well.

On September 25, 1789, Congress proposed a series of amendments to the Constitution. These first ten amendments became known as the Bill of Rights. In 1791, Congress approved the Bill of Rights and it became part of the Constitution. These ten amendments deal mainly with personal rights and freedoms, such as the freedom of speech, the freedom of religion, and the freedom of the press. The tenth amendment ensured states' rights for issues not specifically covered in the Constitution. (To find out more about the Bill of Rights and the Constitution, read another book in this series, *What Makes America America?*)

With the ratification of the Constitution and the adoption of the Bill of Rights, the United States had become more established as a country. Now the people and their leaders had a set of laws to protect them and to guide their actions. As the new country found its way through its first years, it would need a strong leader at its head to govern it. Looking for such a leader, the people turned immediately to the most popular and influential military general of the Revolutionary War: George Washington.

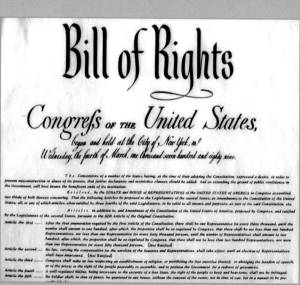

The Bill of Rights

The Bill of Rights

Many of the amendments in the Bill of Rights directly corresponded with injustices done to the American people by the British. They wanted to make very sure such things did not happen again. These are the first four amendments, which deal with individual rights:

I   Congress shall make no law respecting an establishment of religion, or prohibiting the free exercise thereof; or abridging the freedom of speech, or of the press; or the right of the people peaceably to assemble, and to petition the government for a redress of grievances.

II   A well-regulated militia, being necessary to the security of a free state, the right of the people to keep and bear arms, shall not be infringed.

III   No soldier shall, in time of peace be quartered in any house, without the consent of the owner, nor in time of war, but in a manner to be prescribed by law.

IV   The right of the people to be secure in their persons, houses, papers, and effects, against unreasonable searches and seizures, shall not be violated, and no warrants shall issue, but upon probable cause, supported by oath or affirmation, and particularly describing the place to be searched, and the persons or things to be seized.

Mount Vernon, George Washington's home

Five

THE NEW GOVERNMENT

George Washington just wanted to go home. America had won the Revolutionary War, and now he could relax. Throughout the long war, while he had commanded the armies of the United States, he had thought of the lush green fields of his home in Mount Vernon. He fought for America and he fought also for himself, for the chance to return home and live out the rest of his life in peace. On December 23, 1783, the great general resigned his military commission and traveled back to Virginia to begin his retirement. Over the next years, Washington worked on his farm. He made repairs to the house and thought of new ways of producing more crops. People traveled from all over to visit George and Martha Washington, and guests often filled the house.

Washington delighted in his retirement, but he continued to watch events taking place in the new country. What he saw concerned him; the Articles of Confederation were not holding the country together tightly enough. What America needed, Washington wrote to his friend James Madison, was a new, strong constitution.

When the Constitutional Convention began in 1787, Washington arrived to take his place among the Virginia delegates. On the first day, the other delegates unanimously elected him the convention's president. For the next four months, he spent his time in Philadelphia presiding over the creation of the United States Constitution.

After the required nine states had ratified the Constitution, Congress set February 4, 1789, as the date for the first presidential election. Each

*A **cabinet** is a group of advisers.*

George Washington's Mount Vernon

George Washington

state chose its electors, who sent their ballots to Congress after they had voted. When Congress counted the ballots on April 6, they declared George Washington the first President of the United States, by a unanimous sixty-nine electoral votes.

Washington accepted his role as President with good grace, although he questioned his abilities. Martha Washington, too, would have preferred staying at Mount Vernon. Washington felt, however, that he must fulfill the duty his country asked of him, much as he had as commander in chief of the Continental Army. On April 30, 1789, George Washington was inaugurated as the first President of the United States, with John Adams as his Vice President.

Although the Constitution did not require the President to set up a **cabinet**, Washington quickly appointed men to serve under him and advise him on various matters. Thomas Jefferson served as Secretary of State, Alexander Hamilton as Secretary of the

Treasury, Henry Knox as Secretary of War, and Edmund Randolph as Attorney General.

One of the first issues to arise during Washington's presidency concerned a national bank. Alexander Hamilton wanted to create such a bank to shoulder the entire national debt, including the debt held by individual states. Hamilton felt that taking on the national debt in this way would bring the states closer together and strengthen the country. The Northern states, which had more debts, thought a national bank would be a good idea. The Southern states, however, had more money and less debt, and generally did not agree with the plan.

Washington himself wondered whether Hamilton's idea was constitutional. Turning to

George Washington's inauguration as president

Statue of Alexander Hamilton

of the Bank of the United States. He felt that since Hamilton held the position of Secretary of the Treasury, he should be deferred to when a question arose concerning financial matters.

The debate over the national bank created a serious division among leading men in government. Until this time, the United States had no political parties. The Founding Fathers believed political parties would divide the country and make it weaker. Nevertheless, differences in opinion concerning the creation of a national bank led to the beginnings of the two-party system that exists in America today. At the root of the differences lay a disagreement over whether individual states should retain most of the legislative power or if the federal government should take more responsibilities.

Washington did not like the divisions he saw in his cabinet. He worried about the distinct political parties he watched beginning to form. By the end of his first term as President, however, Jefferson's Democratic-Republicans and Hamilton's Federalists had gone from differences in opinion to actual political parties. Time would show that instead of dividing the country, political parties would actually strengthen it by creating a system that closely followed the will of the people. Multiple political parties offered

his cabinet members, he asked for their opinions on the matter. A rift among the cabinet developed, with Hamilton leading those in favor of a national bank and Thomas Jefferson at the head of those who believed the creation of such a bank went against the Constitution. Washington eventually decided to follow Hamilton's suggestion and approve the creation

choices to the American people; if politicians wished to gain votes, they had to act according to the wishes of American citizens.

When the United States took on the national debt with the creation of a national bank, Hamilton proposed a whiskey tax to help pay off that debt. The whiskey tax took effect in 1791, charging large-scale whiskey manufacturers six cents a gallon and small-scale manufacturers nine cents a gallon.

The small farmers of western Pennsylvania were among those hardest hit with the whiskey tax. Many even used whiskey as a form of *currency*. They thought the new tax was extremely unfair, and for a long time they tried to avoid paying at all.

Currency is coins, treasury notes, and bills used as mediums of exchange.

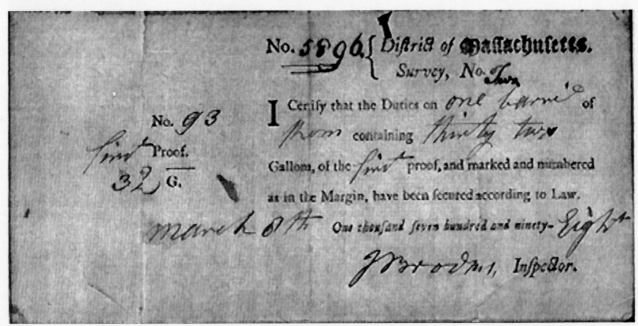

Whiskey tax receipt

Washington led an army to end the Whiskey Rebellion

Tension grew, until finally open rebellion broke out. Angry farmers broke into the houses of tax collectors and forced them to resign their positions. The farmers declared they would obey the laws of their state, but not the laws of the United States. In July of 1794, a mob attacked the house of John Neville, the man who oversaw the local tax collectors. Federal soldiers protecting Neville's house shot and killed one of the rebel leaders during the attack. Infuriated, the farmers returned the next day and burned the buildings on Neville's property. Neville himself fled to safety.

Washington attempted to put down the uprising using local militia, but when this did not work, he personally led an army to end the rebellion. After the arrival of thirteen thousand federal soldiers led by President Washington, the revolt ended quickly with little bloodshed. Washington's unhesitating response sent a clear message to the country about the strength of the national government.

In 1793, the year before the Whiskey Rebellion, France declared war on Britain. During the American Revolution, the United States had signed a treaty with France, and some American leaders thought this treaty should be honored now. Washington, however, knew his country did not have the money or resources to fight a war against Britain again so soon. The United States had just begun trade with Britain once more, which would end if war were declared.

On April 22, 1793, George Washington issued the Neutrality Proclamation, *advocating* "a conduct friendly and *impartial* toward the *belligerent* Powers." Despite America's claim of neutrality, Britain continually boarded American ships and *impressed* sailors into serving in the British navy.

In 1794, Washington sent the Chief Justice, John Jay, to negotiate with the British over the impressment problem, as well as other unresolved issues left over from the end of the Revolutionary War. Jay signed a treaty with the British, but the treaty's only true victory came from the British agreement to abandon their forts on western American land. In return, the treaty gave British companies the right to collect on debts remaining unpaid from before the Revolutionary War. Britain did agree to pay some compensation for the ships and cargoes they had seized, but it made no guarantees that impressments would not continue.

The American people hated the Jay Treaty. They burned effigies of Jay and tried to stone Hamilton as he defended the treaty.

Advocating means supporting; favoring.

Impartial means not having a preference for one thing over another.

Belligerent means war-like.

Impressed means forced.

John Jay

America had given up too much and gotten too little in return, they believed. Not only had Jay failed to resolve all the issues he had been sent to resolve, he had also agreed, on behalf of the United States, that Americans would repay large debts to British companies.

Washington left office in 1797, tired of politics and ready to retire. With the 1797 election, John Adams became President. Thomas Jefferson, who received the second highest number of electoral votes, became his Vice President.

One of the first issues Adams faced as President concerned the continuing war between France and Britain. The Jay Treaty had angered the French as well as the Americans,

since it decidedly favored the British. In their eyes, the treaty violated both the Neutrality Proclamation of 1793 and the earlier Franco-American Treaty of 1778. In response, the French began seizing American ships, claiming they were enemy property and therefore the spoils of war.

Adams determined to resolve the problems with the French. Not long after his inauguration, he sent three men to discuss the matter with the French foreign minister, Tallyrand. When the men arrived in Paris, they asked to speak with Tallyrand. Instead of Tallyrand, however, three Frenchmen arrived, calling themselves only X, Y, and Z. If the Americans wanted to talk directly to Tallyrand, the Frenchmen said, they would have to pay $250,000.

When Americans learned of the XYZ Affair, many wanted to go to war immediately. France had insulted them. Adams did not want to declare war, but what became known as the Quasi-war began, with American ships attacking French ships at sea.

During this period of anti-French feeling in America, the Federalists promoted a group of laws intended to limit the number of immigrants arriving in the United States and becoming American citizens. On July 14, 1798,

Political cartoon portraying the XYZ Affair

Congress passed the Alien and Sedition Acts. The Alien Acts raised the residency requirement for citizenship from five to fourteen years and gave the President the power to *deport* any foreigner he thought could be dangerous. The Sedition Act made it a crime to publish false malicious reports about the government.

*To **deport** means to make someone leave the country.*

Jefferson and the Democratic-Republicans moved to declare the Alien and Sedition Acts unconstitutional. Adams himself had never supported the acts, but their unpopularity led to Jefferson's election in the 1800 presidential election.

Before Adams left office as President, he was able to negotiate the Convention of 1800 with Napoleon, ending all hostilities between America and France. This treaty established the same relationship with France as the Jay Treaty had established with Britain. Most important, it marked the beginning of a diplomatic relationship with France and Napoleon, laying the foundation for the Louisiana Purchase in 1803.

America had grown a great deal since the days of its birth before the Revolutionary War. No longer did Americans see themselves as loyal British subjects. Now they had a nation of their own, with their own constitution, laws, and political system. The young nation still had many questions to resolve over the years—but like a child who grows more mature with each passing birthday, America was becoming stronger as the years passed. It was still more than a century away from being a world power, but it was already proving that it was a force to be respected.

John Adams

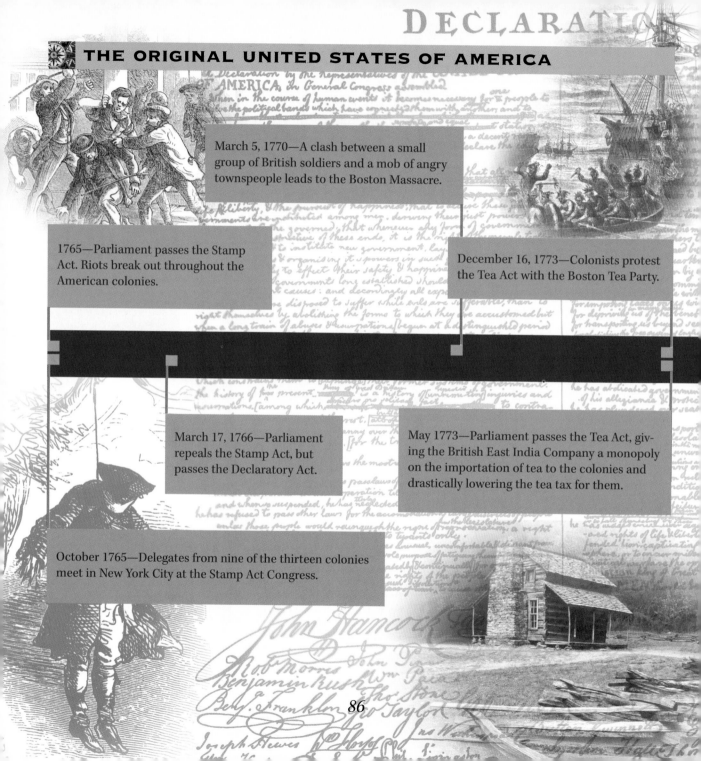

March 5, 1770—A clash between a small group of British soldiers and a mob of angry townspeople leads to the Boston Massacre.

1765—Parliament passes the Stamp Act. Riots break out throughout the American colonies.

December 16, 1773—Colonists protest the Tea Act with the Boston Tea Party.

March 17, 1766—Parliament repeals the Stamp Act, but passes the Declaratory Act.

May 1773—Parliament passes the Tea Act, giving the British East India Company a monopoly on the importation of tea to the colonies and drastically lowering the tea tax for them.

October 1765—Delegates from nine of the thirteen colonies meet in New York City at the Stamp Act Congress.

1774—Parliament passes the Intolerable Acts in retaliation for the Boston Tea Party.

January 1776—Thomas Paine publishes *Common Sense*, calling for America to declare independence from Britain.

April 18, 1775—Paul Revere rides from Boston to rouse the countryside, spreading the news of the British march toward Lexington and Concord; the first battles of the American Revolution begin the next day.

September 1774—The First Continental Congress meets in Philadelphia.

July 4, 1776—The Continental Congress agrees to sign the Declaration of Independence.

May 10, 1775—The Second Continental Congress convenes. They approve the creation of a Continental Army and appoint George Washington as its commander-in-chief.

June 17, 1775—The Battle of Bunker Hill.

87

THE ORIGINAL UNITED STATES OF AMERICA

May 25, 1787—The Constitutional Convention convenes in Philadelphia to write a new Constitution; it is presented to the delegates on September 17.

November 15, 1777—The Continental Congress approves the Articles of Confederation, an early version of the Constitution.

February 4, 1789—The first presidential election unanimously elects George Washington as the first President of the United States. John Adams becomes Vice President.

September 3, 1783—The United States and Britain sign the Treaty of Paris, ending the Revolutionary War. Britain acknowledges the independence of the United States of America.

March 4, 1789—The new United States Constitution goes into effect.

1787—Congress passes the Northwest Ordinance describing the process for new states to join the Union. All new states will have equal rights with existing states.

July 14, 1798—Congress passes the Alien and Sedition Acts, raising residency requirements for American citizenship and making it a crime to publish false and malicious reports about the government.

1794—The Whiskey Rebellion erupts in western Pennsylvania. Washington himself leads the army to quell the uprising, showing the power of the central government.

1791—Congress approves the Bill of Rights, the first ten amendments to the Constitution.

1800—President Adams negotiates the Convention of 1800 with France, ending all hostilities between the two countries.

1797—Washington leaves office. John Adams becomes the second President, with Thomas Jefferson as his Vice President.

FURTHER READING

Carter, Alden R. *At the Forge of Liberty.* New York: Franklin Watts, 1998.

Carter, Alden R. *Birth of the Republic.* New York: Franklin Watts, 1998.

Carter, Alden R. *Colonies in Revolt.* New York: Franklin Watts, 1998.

Dwyer, Frank. *John Adams.* New York: Chelsea House, 1999.

Fritz, Jean. *The Great Little Madison.* New York: G. P. Putnam's Sons, 1999.

Hull, Mary E. *The Boston Tea Party in American History*. Berkeley Heights, N.J.: Enslow Publishers, 1999.

Johnson, Neil. *The Battle of Lexington and Concord.* New York: Four Winds Press, 1992.

Lukes, Bonnie L. *The American Revolution.* San Diego: Lucent Books, 1996.

Murray, Stuart. *American Revoluation.* New York: DK Publishing, 2002.

Nardo, Don. *The American Revolution.* San Diego: KidHaven Press, 2002.

Nardo, Don. *Declaration of Independence: A Model for Individual Rights.* San Diego: Lucent Books, 1999.

Osborne, Mary Pope. *George Washington: Leader of a New Nation.* New York: Dial Books for Young Readers, 1991.

Rappaport, Doreen and Joan Verniero. *Victory or Death: Stories of the American Revolution.* New York: HarperCollins, 2003.

Stewart, Gail B. *Life of a Soldier.* San Diego: Lucent Books, 2003.

FOR MORE INFORMATION

Boston Massacre
www.bostonmassacre.net

Paul Revere
www.paulreverehouse.org

Revolutionary War
www.americanrevwar.homestead.com/files/
Index2

www.kidport.com/RefLib/UsaHistory/America
nRevolution/AmerRevolution

Valley Forge
www.ushistory.org/valleyforge

Continental Congress and Constitutional
Convention
memory.loc.gov/ammem/bdsds/intro01

Publisher's note:
The Web sites listed on this page were active at the time of publication. The publisher is not responsible for Web sites that have changed their addresses or discontinued operation since the date of publication. The publisher will review and update the Web sites upon each reprint.

BIOGRAPHIES

AUTHOR

Sheila Nelson has always been fascinated with history and the lives of historical figures. She enjoys studying history and learning more about the events and people that have shaped our world. Sheila has written several books on history and other subjects. Recently, she completed a master's degree and now lives in Rochester, New York, with her husband and their baby daughter.

SERIES CONSULTANT

Dr. Jack N. Rakove is a professor of history and American studies at Stanford University, where he is director of American studies. The winner of the 1997 Pulitzer Prize in history, Dr. Rakove is the author of *The Unfinished Election of 2000, Constitutional Culture and Democratic Rule,* and *James Madison and the Creation of the American Republic.* He is also the president of the Society for the History of the Early American Republic.

PICTURE CREDITS

Colonial Williamsburg: pp. 16–17, 61
Corel: pp. 38, 56–57, 66–67, 76–77
Dover: cover, pp. 14, 17, 19, 20, 26–27, 30, 33, 37, 43, 44, 48, 51, 54, 55, 57, 78, 86, 86–87, 88–89
The Freedom Trail: pp. 28, 36, 87, 96
Library of Congress: pp. 50, 88
National Archives and Records Administration: pp. 18, 39, 43, 52, 85, 89
Photos.com: pp. 34–35, 86
U.S. Department of Interior: p. 85
Valley Forge: pp. 14, 18, 58

To the best knowledge of the publisher, all other images are in the public domain. If any image has been inadvertently uncredited, please notify Harding House Publishing Service, Vestal, New York 13850, so that rectification can be made for future printings.

Southern Middle Media
5235 Solomon's Island Rd.
Lothian, MD 20711

WITHDRAWN